The **Essential** Buyer's Guide

HONDA
CBR FireBlade

893cc, 918cc, 929cc, 954cc, 998cc, 999cc. 1992 to 2010

Your marque expert:
Peter Henshaw

T0124824

VELOCE PUBLISHING
THE PUBLISHER OF FINE AUTOMOTIVE BOOKS

Also from Veloce –

Essential Buyer's Guide Series
Alfa GT (Booker)
Alfa Romeo Spider Giulia (Booker & Talbott)
Austin Seven (Barker)
BMW GS (Henshaw)
BSA Bantam (Henshaw)
BSA 500 & 650 Twins (Henshaw)
Citroën 2CV (Paxton)
Citroën ID & DS (Heilig)
Corvette C2 1963-1967 (Falconer)
Fiat 500 & 600 (Bobbitt)
Ford Capri (Paxton)
Harley-Davidson Big Twins (Henshaw)
Hinckley Triumph triples & fours 750, 900, 955, 1000, 1050,
  1200 – 1991-2009 (Henshaw)
Honda CBR600 (Henshaw)
Honda FireBlade (Henshaw)
Honda SOHC fours 1969-1984 (Henshaw)
Jaguar E-type 3.8 & 4.2-litre (Crespin)
Jaguar E-type V12 5.3-litre (Crespin)
Jaguar XJ 1995-2003 (Crespin)
Jaguar XK8 (1996-2005) (Thorley)
Jaguar/Daimler XJ6, XJ12 & Sovereign (Crespin)
Jaguar/Daimler XJ40 (Crespin)
Jaguar Mk2 (1955 to 1969) (Thorley)
Jaguar XJ-S (Crespin)
Land Rover Series I, II & IIA (Thurman)
MGB & MGB GT (Williams)
Mercedes-Benz 280SL-560DSL Roadsters (Bass)
Mercedes-Benz 'Pagoda' 230SL, 250SL & 280SL Roadsters
  & Coupés (Bass)
MG Midget & A-H Sprite (Horler)
MG TD, TF & TF1500 (Jones)
Mini (Paxton)
Morris Minor & 1000 (Newell)
Norton Commando (Henshaw)
Peugeot 205 GTi (Blackburn)
Porsche 911 (964) (Streather)
Porsche 911 (993) (Streather)
Porsche 911 (996) (Streather)
Porsche 911 SC (Streather)
Porsche 928 (Hemmings)
Rolls-Royce Silver Shadow & Bentley T-Series (Bobbitt)
Subaru Impreza (Hobbs)
Triumph Bonneville (Henshaw)
Triumph Spitfire & GT6 (Baugues)
Triumph Stag (Mort & Fox)
Triumph TR6 (Williams)

Triumph TR7 & TR8 (Williams)
Vespa Scooters – Classic 2-stroke models 1960-2008
  (Paxton)
VW Beetle (Cservenka & Copping)
VW Bus (Cservenka & Copping)
VW Golf GTI (Cservenka & Copping)

From Veloce Publishing's new imprints:

Soviet General & field rank officer uniforms: 1955 to 1991
  (Streather)
Red & Soviet military & paramilitary services: female uniforms
  1941-1991 (Streather)

Animal Grief – How animals mourn for each other (Alderton)
Clever Dog! (O'Meara)
Complete Dog Massage Manual, The – Gentle Dog Care
  (Robertson)
Dinner with Rover (Paton-Ayre)
Dog Cookies (Schops)
Dog Games – Stimulating play to entertain your dog and
  you (Blenski)
Dogs on wheels (Mort)
Dog Relax – Relaxed dogs, relaxed owners (Pilguj)
Exercising your puppy: a gentle & natural approach – Gentle
  Dog Care (Robertson)
Fun and games for cats (Seidl)
Know Your Dog – The guide to a beautiful relationship
  (Birmelin)
Living with an Older Dog – Gentle Dog Care (Alderton & Hall)
My dog has cruciate ligament injury – but lives life to the full!
  (Häusler)
My dog has hip dysplasia – but lives life to the full! (Häusler)
My dog is blind – but lives life to the full! (Horsky)
My dog is deaf – but lives life to the full! (Willms)
Smellorama – nose games for dogs (Theby)
Swim to Recovery: Canine hydrotherapy healing (Wong)
Waggy Tails & Wheelchairs (Epp)
Walkin' the dog – motorway walks for drivers and dogs
  (Rees)
Winston ... the dog who changed my life (Klute)
You and Your Border Terrier – The Essential Guide (Alderton)
You and Your Cockapoo – The Essential Guide (Alderton)

www.veloce.co.uk

First published in February 2011 by Veloce Publishing Limited, Veloce House, Parkway Farm Business Park, Middle Farm Way,
Poundbury, Dorchester, Dorset, DT1 3AR, England. Fax 01305 250479/
e-mail info@veloce.co.uk/web www.veloce.co.uk or www.velocebooks.com.

ISBN: 978-1-845843-07-6 UPC:6-36847-04307-0

British Library Cataloguing in Publication Data – A catalogue record for this book is available from the British Library.
Typesetting, design and page make-up all by Veloce Publishing Ltd on Apple Mac.
Printed in India by Replika Press.

Introduction
– the purpose of this book

CBR FireBlade – fewer names are more evocative in motorcycling, certainly since the 1990s. Honda's most enduring sports bike deserves every shred of that adulation, and for good reason: it offers race track performance in a road legal bike, yet it will happily potter through town, is civilised and relatively comfortable. Also, if looked after properly the 'Blade is very reliable and capable of serious mileage.

For simplicity we'll refer to the model as the Fireblade or just 'Blade from this point.

When it was launched back in 1992, the FireBlade caused a sensation. Here was a 900cc sports bike, the size and weight of a 600. Lighter than its litre-bike rivals by at least 30kg, it handled like a 600, too. It could rocket through a standing quarter-mile in 10.5 seconds (making it the fastest production bike at the time), and top 166mph. That was the 124bhp original – the latest FireBlades pack 180bhp and are no heavier.

Better still, the FireBlade has always sold in huge numbers, so if you're looking for a secondhand one, there's plenty of choice. If the bike you're looking at has unexplained crash damage, or no service history, or the documentation doesn't match up, then just walk away and find a better one. And being a Honda, this is a quality, well engineered machine with few foibles – another reason to buy secondhand.

This book is a straightforward, practical guide to doing just that. It doesn't list all the correct colour combinations for each year, or delve into the minutae of year-by-year changes (though we have provided a brief guide) – there are books and websites that will supply all of this. Hopefully, it will help you avoid the proverbial lemon, because as with any bike, there are some of those about.

A FireBlade is still one of the most exciting bikes you can buy.

In fact, it's worth remembering that not everyone can cope with the FireBlade's manic performance. With a power-to-weight ratio not far short of a Formula 1 car, it can get the unwary into trouble very quickly. So when looking at a used FireBlade, checking for crash damage has to be top of your list. You might even think twice about buying a 'Blade at all, if it's your first sports bike – a 600 won't scare you quite so easily and could make more sense.

On the other hand, if you do buy a FireBlade, you will be riding one of the milestone sports bikes – pick a decent one, treat it with respect, and you shouldn't regret it. Incidentally, North American readers may be wondering what this 'FireBlade' business is all about, as the name was never officially used in the USA. There, the bike was known by its more prosiac CBR900RR, CBR1000RR, and so on. The bikes, whether or not badged as FireBlades, are the same.

Thanks are due to Roger Maddever, proud owner of a 60,000-mile 'Blade, to Matt Saunders at V&J Honda, and Nick at V&J Suzuki. Also to Honda UK, Annice Collet at the VMCC Library, and to Louise Hillier and Gary Prisk.

Lots of power in a compact lightweight package is the 'Blade's appeal.

The 2008-on 'Blade is a tiny 180bhp projectile.

Essential Buyer's Guide™ currency
At the time of publication a BG unit of currency "●" equals approximately £1.00/US$1.50/Euro 1.20. Please adjust to suit current exchange rates.

Contents

Introduction
– the purpose of this book 3

1 Is it the right bike for you?
– marriage guidance 6

2 Cost considerations
– affordable, or a money pit? 8

3 Living with a FireBlade
– will you get along together? 9

4 Relative values
– which model for you? 11

5 Before you view
– be well informed 17

6 Inspection equipment
– these items will really help 19

7 Fifteen minute evaluation
– walk away or stay? 20

8 Key points
– where to look for problems 22

9 Serious evaluation
– 30 minutes for years of enjoyment .. 23

10 Auctions
– sold! Another way to buy your
dream 46

11 Paperwork
– correct documentation is
essential! 48

12 What's it worth?
– let your head rule your heart 50

13 Do you really want to restore?
– it'll take longer and cost more than
you think 51

14 Paint problems
– bad complexion, including dimples,
pimples and bubbles 53

15 Lack of use problems
– just like their owners, FireBlades
need exercise! 55

16 The Community
– key people, organisations and
companies in the FireBlade world 56

17 Vital statistics
– essential data at your fingertips 57

Index 64

1 Is it the right bike for you?
– marriage guidance

Tall and short riders
The FireBlade is not a big bike physically, so smaller riders needn't worry. In fact, it can feel cramped for six-footers, so try before you buy (though the 1998/99 bikes are roomier).

Running costs
Quite high, but then you're paying the price for supercar-type performance in tyres, chains, and sprockets. Tyre life varies with riding style, but 3000 miles is a good average on the rear, with as much as 7000 on the front. 'Blades can also drink a lot of fuel – expect 40-45mpg ridden gently, 30-40mpg more usually, and less than 30mpg on track days.

Maintenance
No more onerous than many other bikes (4000-mile oil changes) and less so than the equivalent Ducati, but you will need to keep an eye on those consumables. The 16,000-mile service is the major one that includes a valve clearance check.

Usability
Pretty good by sports bike standards. The riding position (early 'Blades excepted) isn't too extreme, the bike is happy to potter around in town, and if you stick to the service schedule, it's reliable as well.

Parts availability
Excellent. Just about everything, for every FireBlade back to 1992, is available from Honda dealers within a few days of ordering – dealers don't keep much in stock though. Bike breakers are a good source of cheaper secondhand parts.

Parts costs
Routine service items – filters, brake pads, and so on – don't cost much, and in the normal run of things, that's all you'll need. But if the bike needs something major, or some crash damage repairing, then life can get expensive. But don't forget the bike breakers for secondhand parts – there's plenty of choice, but be satisfied that the part you're paying for is in good condition from a reputable seller.

Insurance group
High, at group 17 in the UK. The 'Blade's reputation is such that anyone with a poor record (or even worse, aged less than 30) may find it difficult to get insurance at any price. Forty-plus riders with a good record will find it more affordable.

Investment potential
Low, as there are so many around, but it's worth hanging on to the earliest twin-headlamp bikes, while the slightly later 'fox eye' models with the Urban Tiger colour scheme will always be sought after. Later bikes in Repsol colours are favoured too. And if you can find one, a TT100 Evolution FireBlade should have real investment potential.

Foibles
Not many, because it's a Honda! A very well designed, highly developed bike.

Plus points
Stunning performance, superb handling and responses, light weight. It's useable enough to ride on the road every day, yet is a superb tool for track days.

Minus points
Running costs and insurance, riding position is hard on the wrists.

Alternatives
Plenty from Japan. Suzuki's GSX-R750 and 1000, Yamaha R1, and Kawasaki ZX-9R. For something a bit different, try a Ducati 998/999 or Triumph Daytona 955i.

Try before you buy – a FireBlade may not suit.

2 Cost considerations
– affordable, or a money pit?

FireBlades can cost a lot to run, especially if you make full use of the performance or do a lot of miles (or worse still, both). A typical minor service at 4000 miles costs ●x120-130 at a Honda dealer. Insurance costs are high and a rear tyre can last less than 3000 miles, given a hard rider. Fuel consumption can be over 40mpg when ridden smoothly, but 30-40mpg is more typical. Spares prices below are for a year 2000 FireBlade, for genuine Honda parts from either a Honda dealer or an independent specialist.

Rear tyres can last less than 3000 miles.

Air filter element ●x25
Battery ●x40
Brake master cylinder repair kit ●x30
Brake lever ●x25
Front brake pads (set) ●x38
Clutch basket ●x95
Clutch cable ●x15
Clutch lever ●x9
Chain and sprocket kit ●x119
Exhaust downpipes ●x275
Exhaust silencer ●x460
Fairing left-hand lower ●x135
Fairing top ●x210
Fork seal set (per leg) ●x11
Ignition coil/plug gap (ea) ●x35
Oil filter ●x8
Rear shock complete (inc linkage) ●x1041
Starter solenoid ●x49
Tyre (front) ●x77
Tyre (rear) ●x96
Water pump ●x119

A snapped clutch lever is cheap to replace ...

But a silencer, even an aftermarket one, won't be cheap.

3 Living with a FireBlade
– will you get along together?

If you've never owned a sports bike before, think hard before taking the plunge with a FireBlade. These are highly focused machines with just one aim in mind – speed. So it's not a cossetting sort of bike. You perch on, not sit in, the FireBlade, and the riding position (especially on early bikes) is quite uncompromising, with lots of weight on your wrists, shoulders and neck, which can be a literal pain at low speeds. Actually, by sports bike standards, in this respect the FireBlade isn't too bad, and certainly a lot more comfy than some, but it's worth bearing in mind. Over 80mph of course, it all comes together as wind pressure takes the weight off your upper body, but how often will you want to risk your licence?

And not just your licence. FireBlades have a very high power-to-weight ratio plus a short wheelbase, so they are very easy to wheelie, whether intentionally or not! This can catch out the unwary. Early FireBlades in particular have a skittish, light front end which can lead to 'tank slappers' at speed, and many have ended up in hedges, or worse. Later bikes, especially those with the electronic steering damper fitted from 2004, are less wild, more controllable.

In fact, after trying a FireBlade you might find it's not the bike for you anyway. If so, consider the alternatives. Sticking to Honda, a CBR600 offers something of the same adrenalin rush, but is a much more sensible choice for the first-time sports bike buyer – it's cheaper to run, too. If you do a lot of miles two-up, then a sports tourer like the VFR800 will make a lot more sense, and be kinder to the pillion.

On the other hand, you may find the niggles a price well worth paying in exchange for the sheer excitement and concentrated riding experience that a FireBlade can deliver. Indeed, that massive power and uncompromising nature is all part of the bike's appeal. And it is a beguiling package, the size of a 600 or 750, but with a lot more torque. It is a fantastic piece of kit with a near race bike character, and which can only really be given its head on a track day. If you want to ride fast on a circuit, then a FireBlade is a good bike to do it on, so long as you treat it with respect. The bike is capable of delivering far more power than most riders can handle.

The pillion seat is relatively comfy on the early bikes.

In any case, as sports bikes go, the 'Blade is relatively easy to ride, happy to trickle along at town speeds (even if your wrists aren't!) – compared to something like a Ducati, it's positively civilised – and more comfortable than many contemporary sports bikes. Some riders even go touring on them, so it can be done, though you'll have to strap on some soft luggage.

Despite offering supercar levels of performance, and a redline at 10-12,000rpm, the FireBlade doesn't need constant and intricate maintenance. This is a Honda after all, a quality bike designed to deliver performance consistently so long as the maintenance schedule is kept to. That means a minor service (oil, filter, etc) at 4000 miles, which for most riders will mean once a year, as sports bikes tend not to be used for day-to-day commuting. There's an intermediate service at 8000 (with a sparkplug change) and a major at 16,000 which includes a valve clearance check, but that's about it.

So, maintenance is straightforward, but you will need to keep a close eye on consumables. The laws of physics dictate that a bike this fast and powerful is capable of getting through tyres, chains, sprockets and brake pads scarily quickly. Of course, it all depends on how you ride. Most owners should expect 3000 miles out of a rear tyre, and some smooth riding types will get more, but those who like to make the most of the bike's potential, whether on the road or track days, will see a lot less. And the same goes for chains, sprockets, and pads – wheelies in particular are bad news for chain and sprocket life.

As for fuel consumption, ride a FireBlade gently, and it's possible to return 40-45mpg; but use that power, and expect it to dip to 30mpg or below (even 20mpg on a track day). The bottom line is that speed costs money, but as with the riding position, it may be a price you're prepared to pay for the riding experience.

Mind you, the price could be higher still if the bike 'disappears.' It's a sad fact of life that FireBlades are quite stealable. Honda fitted a decent steering lock, and from 1998 an electronic immobiliser, but the 'Blade has always been attractive to thieves thanks to its light weight and ready saleability. And there are so many around that it's relatively easy to give one a false identity, or break it for spares. When buying, check that the engine and frame numbers tally with the registration document, and use an HPI check on the bike's history. And if you've bought it, keep the bike safe with your own security measures, both at home and out in the world.

Finally, insurance. FireBlades are labelled high-risk bikes because of their performance, stealability and crash record. That means very high premiums if you are young or have a poor driving record. Well behaved middle-aged riders will be able to insure the 'Blade for a far more reasonable sum (especially compared to a sports car with similar performance), but either way, it's worth getting a few quotes before deciding to buy one.

The FireBlade is not an everyday, all year round sort of bike, but treat it as the uncompromising performance tool that it is, and it will deliver an unforgettable riding experience. Just remember who's in charge ...

FireBlade ownership requires some commitment.

4 Relative values
– which model for you?

See chapter 12 for value assessment. This chapter shows, in relative percentage terms, the value of individual models in good condition relative to a year 2000 'Blade. This chapter looks at the strengths and weaknesses of each model, so that you can decide which is best for you. Generally, the FireBlade got calmer and more civilised over the years, but from 2000 onwards combined that refinement with ever more power and less weight in an increasingly compact package. Honda has tended to give the bike major updates ever couple of years, but I've organised it around four eras, based on significant engine changes. Because there were so many changes over the years, it's worth noting that the 2010 bike has nothing in common with the '92 original, apart from the name, concept, and basic layout.

Range availability

Year	Model	cc		Year	Model	cc
1992	CBR900RR-N	893cc		2001	CBR900RR-1	929cc
1993	CBR900RR-P	893cc		2002	CBR900RR-2	954cc
1994	CBR900RR-R	893cc		2003	CBR900RR-3	954cc
1995	CBR900RR-S	893cc				
				2004	CBR1000RR-4	998cc
1996	CBR900RR-T	918cc		2005	CBR1000RR-5	998cc
1997	CBR900RR-V	918cc		2006	CBR1000RR-6	998cc
1998	CBR900RR-W	918cc		2007	CBR1000RR-7	998cc
1999	CBR900RR-X	918cc		2008	CBR1000RR-8	1000cc
				2009	CBR1000RR-9	1000cc
2000	CBR900RR-Y	929cc		2010	CBR1000RR-10	1000cc

1992-1995

The original FireBlades of 1992/93 were the wildest of all, gaining a reputation as fearsome racers for the road, liable to spit off or tank slap the unwary. They certainly do offer the FireBlade experience in its most raw and elemental form. Pared to the

bone, they weigh just 185kg, allowing the 124bhp liquid-cooled four-cylinder engine to give stunning performance. Torquey compared to contemporary 750s, they actually offered little at low revs, taking off like the proverbial scalded cat through the upper half of the rev range. A 16in front wheel and sharp geometry meant very quick steering, but the front end was a little too light, with harsh damping – exciting stuff, but it could lead to tank slappers which the bike might or might not ride through.

The '93 'Blade was much the same, and these earliest bikes, with their twin round

The original, and for some the best, but early 'Blades are a wild ride.

headlights, are becoming collectors' items – not many have survived, and even fewer in original form, as 'Blade owners loved adding accessories; everything from coloured screens, to steering dampers (a good idea), to race cans. Early 'Blades, contrary to their wild image, also offered more underseat space than any contemporary sports bike.

If you can find an early bike as unmarked and original as this, it's worth buying.

For 1994, Honda calmed the 'Blade down a little. Engine power was unchanged, but the handling was softened by a 180/55 rear tyre (replacing a 160/60) and revised 45mm forks with better damping – the rear shock got more effective damping as well. The gearbox was improved (it was a bit clunky on the early bikes) and the '94 bike was instantly recognisable by its sleeker one-piece headlight, the 'fox eye,' and a taller screen. Another eye catching change was the orange and brown 'Urban Tiger' colour scheme, only offered for 1994 and now widely regarded as one of the classic FireBlade colours. There were few changes for '95, apart from a slightly taller 800mm seat to relax the riding position a little.

Strengths/weaknesses:
• Raw riding experience from the 92/93 bikes, tamed somewhat for 94/95.
• 'Blades this old may have had a hard life, and the ride is a bit too wild for some, though the ultimate adrenalin rush for others.

1992 – **51%** 1993 – **56%** 1994 – **61%** 1995 – **66%**

1996-1999

These were relatively relaxed years for the FireBlade – Honda was surprised by demand for the bike, and decided to make it softer and easier to ride, thus accessible for more riders. To put this in context, the 'Blade was still a very fast,

sharp steering sports bike, but now it was more comfortable and less demanding – the '98/99 machines are thought to make decent sports tourers, but with more of an edge than a VFR800.

Central to the second generation 'Blade was a new 918cc engine, with 128bhp and a more useable spread of power. The bottom end was stronger, as was the clutch, and the

Second generation 'Blades are bigger and softer.

The soft reputation of 1997/98 means you could bag a bargain.

new motor sat in a new twin-spar triple box section frame with a more robust swingarm. The riding position was more relaxed and upright, and the suspension upgraded. The only significant change for 1997 was an aluminium silencer, saving a small amount of weight.

For '98, the FireBlade went softer still, with revised geometry (offsetting the fork yokes by 5mm) to tame the front end. Power was unchanged, but new carb slides and remapped ignition improved torque at low speed. With better suspension and greater refinement, this was the comfiest 'Blade yet, and actually lighter, at 180kg, than its predecessor despite being physically bigger. Lower drag was claimed for the redesigned fairing, which gave more weather protection. Honda's electronic immobiliser (HISS) came as standard, as did a fully electronic instrument panel.

There were new front brake calipers and larger (310mm) front discs, plus a tapered box section swingarm claimed to be more rigid than before. There was a special edition 'Blade in '98, to celebrate Honda's 50th anniversary in the motorcycle business – mechanically unchanged, but with a red/white colour scheme, and a '50th Anniversary' plaque on the top yoke. There were no significant changes for '99.

One 1998 bike worth seeking out (though you'll have to look hard) is the TT100 Evolution FireBlade. Honda wanted to beat the Yamaha R1 on the Isle of Man, which meant building 150 special editions to homologate an upgraded 'Blade for Production racing. Developed by tuner Russell Savory and Mick Grant, the Evo offered 165bhp from its highly tuned engine, a close-ratio gearbox and four-into-one titanium exhaust. There were Ohlins racing forks and rear shock, a single-sided swingarm and Brembo racing brakes, all enveloped in new bodywork (though it still looked like a FireBlade) from renowned stylist John Keogh. But official protests meant that the bike never raced, and not many were built. Still, it makes for a real collector's item today.

Strengths/weaknesses:
• Derided by purists for going soft, the '95-'99 'Blades have a lot to offer. They are the best all-rounders (though physically large in '98/99) and cheaper than new bikes, plus more available than the earliest machines.
• As with all older 'Blades, you'll have to search hard to find a standard one.
• Evo 'Blade is a real collector's piece, and won't be cheap.

1996 – **71%** 1997 – **77%** 1998 – **80%** 1999 – **85%**

2000-2003
With new competition from Yamaha's R1 and Kawaski's latest ZX-9R, Honda had

Radical changes for 2000 brought the 'Blade back up to speed.

to do something drastic to the FireBlade for 2000, and it did. The Millennium 'Blade was 10kg lighter than the '99, but with significantly more power and torque – 152bhp and 76lb ft. That was down to a new 929cc engine with electronic fuel injection, as the 'Blade finally ditched its carbs. It also had a bypass starter for quicker and easier firing up, and a new exhaust with H-TEV (it stood for Honda Titanium Exhaust Valve).

Chassis-wise, the most significant change was the adoption of a 17in front wheel (with wider tyre) in place of the old 16in, plus upside down forks, both of them long-awaited by 'Blade enthusiasts. The redesigned twin-spar frame was claimed to be lighter and stiffer than before, and came with a new swingarm. The seat was higher, at 815mm, the HISS immobiliser improved, and the styling was sharper, though some thought it looked less individual than the old 'Blade. Three-spoke wheels are a recognition point compared to older 'Blades. The '01 was little changed, and both were known as CBR929RR in the USA.

Once again, the new bike was easier to ride and more civilised than the old, and some magazine tests marked the 'Blade down against the excitement of the R1 or Suzuki's new GSX-R1000. But the Honda continued to outsell its rivals in the key sports bike market of the UK, simply because its performance was more accessible and less scary. For purists, it was at the sports-tourer end of the sports bike market, but for many more riders, this all-round appeal made it the bike of choice.

2002 saw another capacity hike, this time to 954cc and with bigger fuel injectors, though according to the official figures max power was actually down slightly at 154bhp, and torque up to 77lbt ft. The frame and headstock were stronger than before, and the swingarm more rigid, despite which the '02 'Blade was actually 2kg lighter than the '01 – a dry weight of 168kg made it lighter than every other litre sports bike, not to mention Honda's own CBR600. But the most obvious change was the striking new styling and headlight. There were new colours in 2003, but not much else.

Strengths/weaknesses:
• The refinement process continued, but the 'Blade also lost some weight and bulk, underlining the bike's all-rounder status amongst sports bikes.
• The GSX-R1000 was arguably closer to the concept of the wild old 'Blade, but this latest version suited most riders better.

2000 – **100%** 2001 – **107%** 2002 – **134%** 2003 – **143%**

2004-2010
The latest generation FireBlade was all-new for 2004, widely anticipated and

disappointing no one. Despite being new from front to back, the CBR1000RR continued the process the 'Blade had been undergoing since 2000 – extra refinement while continuing to increase power, reduce weight and sharpen the handling.

The new diecast frame had similar architecture to that of Honda's RCV MotoGP bike, with the rear shock and linkage mounted to the swingarm, hence no upper link. The engine boosted power and torque significantly to 178bhp/85lb ft, thanks to a capacity rise to 998cc, two-stage fuel injection and ram air induction, plus lighter internals for faster revving. It was also shorter, and so mounted further forward, benefiting weight distribution and allowing a longer swingarm without lengthening the wheelbase – both these changes stabilised the handling. One clever new feature was the electronic steering damper, which automatically changed the damping force according to speed – it still featured on FireBlades in 2010, and worked very well and unobtrusively. The front brake calipers were now radially mounted, and the discs were smaller (310mm) and thus lighter, while road testers agreed that the new brakes were very powerful with lots of feel. The bigger 140mm clutch was now hydraulic, not cable, and a new instrument display included a gearshift indicator. As well as new styling, another instantly recognisable point was the underseat stainless steel exhaust – in the fashion of the time, but it stole underseat space. At 179kg, the 2004 FireBlade was 11kg heavier than the old generation, but the huge margin of power and torque more than made up for that.

Once again, road testers raved, as the new 'Blade made high speed easier to access than ever before, coupling that with plenty of feedback, fine brakes, grippy tyres and that electronic steering damper. They made the point that, unlike a GSX-R1000, the 'Blade didn't need every ounce of concentration to keep it under control.

There were few mechanical changes the following year, but 2005 did see the arrival of limited edition Repsol colours, and the red/white/blue HRC colour scheme. The Repsol became the colour to have for many, with its strong racing connections, and Honda offered the scheme every other year as an option. 2006 saw detail changes to the engine (a higher rev limit but not more power), plus new clutch bearings, revised geometry, and larger 320mm front discs.

2004 saw the modern generation bike debut – this is an '05.

All-new bodywork had more aggressive styling. There was recall that year, as some bikes had a too-short fuel pipe – this should have been rectified by now, but any Honda dealer can check that for you.

In keeping with Honda's practice of major changes every two years, there were few for 2007, though the underseat exhaust gained a catalyst (and lost weight), the radiator was smaller and lighter, a 42-tooth rear sprocket lowered the gearing for better acceleration, and geometry was revised to reduce steering effort.

Underseat exhaust marks out the 2004-07 bikes.

It followed that 2008 would bring in big changes, and it did. The engine was now up to 999.8cc, and with no separate cylinder liners (to reduce weight). Power was up to 180bhp and the bike was 6kg lighter than before, giving the best power-to-weight ratio in the litre-bike class. The 'Blade lost its underseat exhaust in favour of a very short, stubby underslung silencer – early examples of these were a bit too hot for the rider's feet, but that was soon rectified by an exhaust cover. And some 2008 bikes, with the liner-less engine, could use a lot of oil, though that too was soon cured. A slipper clutch was now standard, allowing clutch-free down changes, and the electronic steering damper was revised. The bikes also gained a sophisticated self-diagnostic system.

The big news for 2009 was optional ABS, the first time anti-lock brakes had been offered on a sports bike. Honda was very proud of the fact that they added less than a kilo in weight, and emphasised that the system had been carefully designed to suit fast road and track riding. It was a clever system that also limited forward pitching and rear wheel lift under heavy braking. It's easy to spot an ABS-equipped bike – it has metallic bronze calipers, where the standard bikes are black. Few riders took the option in 2009 (the UK price was an extra ⬤x500) but many more did the following year. In '09, the ABS bikes came in HRC colours, with Repsol and metallic black or blue as options.

The 2010 FireBlade is the lightest, fastest, most powerful yet.

There were few big changes for 2010. Repsol colours continued as an option, and one special edition was the HM Plant John McGuinness FireBlade, built to celebrate his status as fastest man around the TT course. The bike had a two-tone paint job, with maps of the TT course on fairing and seat cowl, and each one was autographed by Mr McGuinness.

Strengths/weaknesses:
• Smaller, lighter and more powerful than ever before, the FireBlade took its original philosophy to new heights.
• The sophistication of these latest 'Blades means there is more to go wrong.
• They are far more expensive to buy than an early model.
• Tall riders might find them a little cramped.

2004 – **170%** 2005 – **186%** 2006 – **209%** 2007 – **225%** 2008 – **254%**
2009 – **278%**

5 Before you view
– be well informed

To avoid a wasted journey, and the disappointment of finding that the bike does not match your expectations, it will help if you're very clear about what questions you want to ask before you pick up the phone. Some of these points might appear basic, but when you're excited about the prospect of buying your dream FireBlade, it's amazing how some of the most obvious things slip the mind ... Also check the current values of the model you are interested in in the classified ads.

Where is the bike?
Is it going to be worth travelling to the next county/state, or even across a border? A locally advertised machine, although it may not sound very interesting, can add to your knowledge for very little effort, so make a visit – it might even be in better condition than expected.

Dealer or private sale?
Establish early on if the bike is being sold by its owner or by a trader. A private owner should have all the history, so don't be afraid to ask detailed questions. A dealer may have more limited knowledge of the bike's history, but should have some documentation. A dealer may offer a warranty/guarantee (ask for a printed copy).

Cost of collection and delivery?
A dealer may well be used to quoting for delivery. A private owner may agree to meet you halfway, but only agree to this after you have seen the bike at the vendor's address to validate the documents. Conversely, you could meet halfway and agree the sale, but insist on meeting at the vendor's address for the handover.

View – when and where?
It is always preferable to view at the vendor's home or business premises. In the case of a private sale, the bike's documentation should tally with the vendor's name and address. Arrange to view only in daylight, and avoid a wet day – the vendor may be reluctant to let you take a test ride if it's wet.

Reason for sale?
Do make it one of the first questions. Why is the bike being sold and how long has it been with the current owner? How many previous owners?

Condition?
Ask for an honest appraisal of the bike's condition. Ask specifically about some of the check items described in chapter 8.

All original specification?
FireBlade owners love to fit accessories, and old bikes especially are unlikely to have the original silencer. Braided brake hoses are a good sign, and many owners fit things like belly screens and tinted screens. If the original screen, silencer, etc come as part of the deal, so much the better. If an older bike is completely original, then that's quite a find, though it won't make a huge difference to the value.

Matching data/legal ownership

Do frame, engine numbers and licence plate match the official registration document? Is the owner's name and address recorded in the official registration documents?

For those countries that require an annual test of roadworthiness, does the bike have a document showing it complies (an MoT certificate in the UK, which can be verified on 0845 600 5977)?

Does the bike carry a current road fund license/license plate tag? No FireBlade is old enough to qualify for tax exempt status in the UK.

Does the vendor own the bike outright? Money might be owed to a finance company or bank: the bike could even be stolen. Several organisations will supply the data on ownership, based on the bike's licence plate number, for a fee. Such companies can often also tell you whether the bike has been 'written off' by an insurance company. In the UK these organisations can supply vehicle data:
HPI – 01722 422 422 – www.hpicheck.com
AA – 0870 600 0836 – www.theaa.com
RAC – 0870 533 3660 – www.rac.co.uk
Other countries will have similar organisations.

Insurance

Check with your existing insurer before setting out – your current policy might not cover you if you do buy the bike and decide to ride it home.

How you can pay

A cheque/check will take several days to clear and the seller may prefer to sell to a cash buyer. However, a banker's draft (a cheque issued by a bank) is as good as cash, but safer, so contact your own bank and become familiar with the formalities that are necessary to obtain one.

Buying at auction?

If the intention is to buy at auction see chapter 10 for further advice.

Professional vehicle check (mechanical examination)

In the UK, the AA and RAC no longer perform used motorcycle checks. A Honda dealer or independent specialist may be willing to check a bike over for a fee, but you'll need to get the owner's permission first.

6 Inspection equipment

– these items will really help

This book
Reading glasses (if you need them for close work)
Overalls
Digital camera
Paddock stand
A friend, preferably a knowledgeable enthusiast

Before you rush out of the door, gather together a few items that will help as you work your way around the bike. This book is designed to be your guide at ever step, so take it along and use the check boxes in chapter 9 to help you assess each area of the bike. Don't be afraid to let the seller see you using it.

Taking your reading glasses if you need them to read documents and make close-up inspections.

Be prepared to get dirty. Take along a pair of overalls, if you have them. A digital camera is handy so that later you can study some areas of the bike more closely. Take a picture of any part of the bike that causes you concern, and seek an expert opinion.

A paddock stand is especially useful, and many owners will already have one. By propping up either end of the bike, it makes checking of tyres, chain, sprockets and wheel bearings far more easy.

Ideally, have a friend or knowledgeable enthusiast come along with you to see the bike – a second opinion is always worth having.

www.velocebooks.com / www.veloce.co.uk
All current books • New book news • Special offers • Gift vouchers

Documentation

If the seller claims to be the bike's owner, make sure he/she really is by checking the registration document, which in the UK is V5C. The person listed on the document isn't necessarily the legal owner, but their details should match those of whoever is selling the bike. Also use the document to check the engine/frame numbers.

An annual roadworthiness certificate – the 'MoT' in the UK – is not just handy proof that the bike was roadworthy when tested. A whole sheaf of them gives evidence of the bike's history – when it was actively being used, and what the mileage was. The more of these that come with the bike, the better. Ask for any service history as well – routine servicing, repairs and recalls.

Engine/frame numbers

Does the VIN (Vehicle Identification Number) and engine number tally with those on the documentation? The VIN plate is on the left- or right-hand upper frame spar, just in front of the fuel tank, and the engine number is on top of the gearbox, just inward of the clutch cable lever, though this is very difficult to see on later bikes. Do the numbers look original; not tampered with?

If the numbers don't tally, you may just be looking at a bike that has had an engine swap that was never recorded in the paperwork, or it could have been built up from stolen parts. If the

The VIN plate information should confirm the bike's age, and match that on the documents.

owner can't come up with a convincing explanation, walk away – there are plenty of legitimate FireBlades to choose from.

General condition

With the bike outside and in good light, take a good, slow walk around it. If it's claimed to be restored, and has a nice shiny tank and engine cases, look more closely – how far does the 'restored' finish go? Are the nooks and crannies behind the gearbox as spotless as the fuel tank? If not, the bike may have been given a quick smarten up to sell. A generally faded look all over isn't necessarily a bad thing – it suggests a machine that hasn't been restored, and isn't trying to pretend that it has.

The most crucial thing to look for on any FireBlade is evidence of crash damage, or whether it's been raced? Is the bodywork unmarked, or suspiciously new on an otherwise tatty bike? When a bike does hit the deck, the same things suffer almost every time, so take a good look at the

Chewed up fasteners are a sign of misuse.

silencer, footrests, mirrors, indicators, levers and bar ends for signs of trips down the road. Plastic bodywork protectors can be bent or scratched (though they're very easy to replace). Scraped engine or clutch cases (or even worse, holed cases, hastily patched up with resin) are confirmation of a hard life.

Check the frame for crash damage.

Engine/suspension/tyres

Check the engine oil, via a dipstick on 1992-94 bikes, or a window below the clutch cover from 1995 – both on the right hand side of the engine. Is it at the correct level? No metal particles floating around? Start the engine. It should fire up promptly and rev up crisp and clean. Blip the throttle and watch for blue smoke, a sign of top-end wear. Have a listen – a rattle at idle could be a problem with the camchain tensioner, and any knocks or rumbles are signs of serious camshaft or bearing wear.

Tyres and chain are other indicators of whether the owner is a caring type or

not. Are the tyres worn right round to the sidewalls, or just in the centre? Well worn rubber is a good bargaining counter. Now look at the chain – is it properly adjusted and nicely lubed up? Is the rear sprocket in good condition? If not, take the cost of replacements into account.

Check the front forks for oil leaks, and with the bike propped up check them for play by grasping the bottom of the legs and trying to rock them back and forth. With the front wheel back on the ground and the front brake on, pump the forks up and down – they should move smoothly and without squeaks or rattles.

Sit on the bike and check the rear suspension – as with the forks, the shock should move smoothly and quietly. If it feels oversoft, then it could need replacing.

Tyres are easy to check, and this one's well worn.

8 Key points
– where to look for problems

1. Are screw/bolt heads chewed or rounded-off? Is there damage to casings around fixings? Has someone attacked the fixings with a hammer and chisel? All are sure signs of a careless previous owner with more enthusiasm than skill, coupled with a dash of youthful impatience. Not a good sign ...

2. Check for evidence of crash damage. Not just obviously scraped bodywork, but the engine and clutch casings, the silencer, footpegs, indicators, mirrors and levers. If any of these are newer and shinier than the rest of the bike, that's an indication.

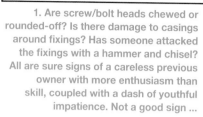

3. Does the mileage on the speedo tally with the bike's overall condition? Mileages tend to be low, as many FireBlades are used as summer-only bikes. A cared-for 30,000-miler is still preferable, however, to a neglected 20,000-miler.

4. Check engine and VIN numbers against documentation – these will confirm who owns the bike, and whether it really is the model and year it's claiming to be.

5. Thin, scored discs are a sign of hard use and neglect. If the discs are newish on an older bike, that's a good sign.

9 Serious evaluation
– 30 minutes for years of enjoyment

Score each section as follows: 4 = excellent; 3 = good; 2 = average; 1 = poor
The totting up procedure is detailed at the end of the chapter. Be realistic in your marking!

The VIN plate is rivetted to the frame.

The engine number is on top of gearbox – this is a 1993 bike.

The VIN/frame number should also be stamped on the headstock.

[4] [3] [2] [1]

Engine/frame numbers

Engine and frame numbers are mentioned several times in this book, and with good reason – there's no better way to check a bike's bona fides. The engine number is on the right-hand side, on top of the gearbox, just behind the clutch cable arm. It may not be visible on later bikes, but you will always be able to find the VIN (or frame number) plate. This is riveted to the frame just in front of the fuel tank, on right-hand on early bikes, the left on later ones. The frame number may also be stamped on the headstock.

Have a good look at the numbers. Do they look as if they've been tampered with? If so, walk away. The quickest way to change a stolen bike's identity is to try and change the numbers.

Check the engine

and frame numbers against those on the documentation – if they're not identical, then the bike is not what the seller says it is. Finally, check the engine and frame prefixes against the table below – these should confirm that both engine and frame are the same year recorded on the registration documents (but note 1992-95 bikes had the same prefixes). If you find that the engine and frame are a year or two apart, there may be a legitimate reason – a secondhand replacement engine, for example – and the result could still be a perfectly fine bike. But the numbers must be as recorded on the paperwork, and non-originality should be reflected in the price. Replacement engines or frames aren't unheard of, but very rare – if the seller gives this as the explanation, ask to see receipts.

The bottom line is, if in doubt, walk away. There are lots secondhand FireBlades around, and most of them have nothing serious to hide.

Year	Engine number prefix	Frame number prefix
1992 (RR-N)	SC28E-	SC28
1993 (RR-P)	SC28E-	SC28
1994 (RR-R)	SC28E-	SC28
1995 (RR-S)	SC28E-	SC28
1996 (RR-T)	SC33E-	SC33A-TM
1997 (RR-V)	SC33E-	SC33A-VM
1998 (RR-W)	SC33E	SC33A-WM
1999 (RR-X)	SC33E	SC33A-XM
2000 (RR-Y)	SC44E	SC44A-YM
2001 (RR-1)	SC44E	SC44A-1M
2002 (RR-2)	SC50E	SC50A-2M
2003 (RR-3)	SC54E	SC54A-3M
2004 (RR-4)	SC57E	SC57A-4M
2005 (RR-5)	SC57E	SC57A-5M
2006 (RR-6)	SC57E	SC57A-6M
2007 (RR-7)	SC57E	SC57A-7M
2008 (RR-8)	SC57E	SC57A-8M
2009 (RR-9)	SC57E	SC57A-9M

Paint/chrome/alloy

Honda's paint finish is good,but as on any bike it is susceptible to neglect. The fuel tank may have been worn by crouching riders over the years, but many owners add stick-on pads to prevent this.

Take a look at the fairing sides for scratch damage – a gentle slide down the road may have left the bodywork intact but made a real mess of the paintwork or decals. Fairing colour schemes are a big part of any 'Blade's appeal, but particularly desirable ones, such as the early Urban Tiger or later Repsol colours. Fairings can be repainted and decals replaced, but it all takes time and money, so again, damage here should be reflected in the price.

Old but well-kept alloy.

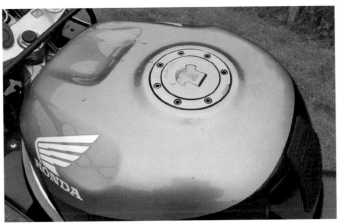

Honda's paint finish is decent quality, but keep an eye open for scrapes and scratches.

There's very little chrome on a FireBlade, but lots of alloy. As with the paintwork, Honda's finish is pretty good quality, but the bike only needs to be left unwashed after a couple of salty rides for corrosion to take hold – plating comes off alloy and steel parts rust. This affects all bikes, though obviously the older they are the more they are likely to have suffered, and it needs a meticulous owner to to have washed the bike after every winter ride.

Check the engine cases for peeling or bubbling lacquer, and all alloy parts for corrosion. None of this affects how the bike goes, but it looks unsightly and does have an effect on value, if only because many FireBlades have been summer use only bikes that haven't suffered from winter corrosion. If you do decide to ignore the corrosion and bag yourself a bargain, don't forget that it will be more difficult to sell on.

Bodywork

In one respect, buying a secondhand bike is far easier than purchasing a used car – there's far less bodywork to worry about. The quality of Honda's plastic is pretty good, though it will still suffer if the bike has been dropped. The panels should be secure on the bike – Dzu fastners on pre-1999 bikes, allen screws on later ones.

Many owners fit plastic bodywork protectors, which do a good job if the bike does go down. Check these aren't scraped or bent. If they are overtightened, these can crack the castings they're bolted onto.

If the fairing is cracked or badly scraped, new Honda replacements aren't cheap, though most are available, complete with the correct decals already in place. Bike breakers are a good source of secondhand panels, of which there's a reasonable supply.

So cracked plastic is no reason to reject a bike, as long as the damage is reflected in the price, and you are prepared to search for a replacement and fit it – it may also need repainting to match the rest of the bike. One alternative to a breakers is aftermarket bodywork, cheaper than Honda's own.

Either way, a new looking fairing on an otherwise shabby bike suggests it has been crashed. Not that many FireBlades have been raced, but racers sometimes fit cheap panels to save the originals. Track day use is far more common ... and so is the ensuing damage!

Badges/ decals

   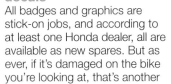

All badges and graphics are stick-on jobs, and according to at least one Honda dealer, all are available as new spares. But as ever, if it's damaged on the bike you're looking at, that's another

Bodywork and decals are easily checked for damage. Honda can supply replacements.

Check crash buttons/bungs for damage, too.

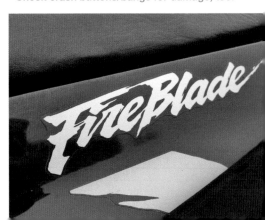

New decals are available ...

good lever to get the price down. Peeling off old graphics, and getting new ones in the right place without creases or bubbles, is never as straightforward as it seems.

... and they're part of a 'Blade's appeal.

Seat

All FireBlades have separate solo and pillion seats, though the passenger's perch is sometimes hidden by a cowling. As with any seat, check for splits and tears; this doesn't just look tatty, it also allows rain water in, which the foam padding soaks up ...

Rider's seat – can you spot the repair?

Insulation tape will cover small splits ...

and never dries out. Recovering is the only answer, something which any motorcycle seat specialist can do, and as these aren't big items, it shouldn't cost much either. It's possible the pillion seat is unlikely to have seen much use!

Footrests

Worn footrests are a good indication of mileage, though of course they are quite easy and cheap to replace – if they are noticeably newer and shinier than the rest of the bike, that's a sure sign they have been. Check the footrest protectors, otherwise known as 'hero blobs,' underneath the rests – if they are

Worn footrest rubbers betray high mileage.

scraped that's a sign of a hard, enthusiastic rider, though that's not necessarily a bad thing. Don't forget the pillion rests as well.

Frame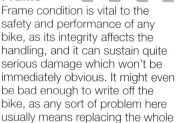

Frame condition is vital to the safety and performance of any bike, as its integrity affects the handling, and it can sustain quite serious damage which won't be immediately obvious. It might even be bad enough to write off the bike, as any sort of problem here usually means replacing the whole frame – that's sometimes more than the entire bike is worth.

The good news is that all FireBlade frames are well made and very strong, built to take the sort of abuse that sports bikes can suffer from. Your difficulty as a buyer is that it's not easy to examine every inch of the frame. What you can do is use a straight edge to check that the wheels are in line (though a problem here could simply be a misaligned rear wheel), and the visible parts of the main frame spars for dents (watch for strategically-placed carbon fibre strips stuck on to hide them). With the handlebars on full lock, have a look at the headstock – after the forks, this takes the brunt of any head-on collision, so check for any signs of damage here. Check the steering stops, the little lugs that limit handlebar movement. If they are damaged, that's a sign of a crash – they may even have snapped off altogether.

Take off the seat to examine the rear subframe, and if the owner's agreeable, remove the fuel tank (two bolts – you shouldn't need to disconnect the fuel pipe) to have a look at the main frame underneath. The owner may allow you to take some fairing panels off as well (easier on pre-1999 bikes, with their Dzu fasteners), but don't count on it.

Finally, when out on the test ride check that the bike runs in a straight line (though again, veering to one side could just be down to rear wheel alignment), and responds well to steering input.

The headstock suffers in a head-on collison.

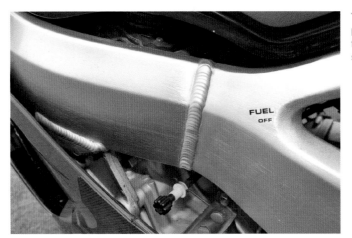

This frame is pristine – check for dents and scrapes.

Check that the side stand is secure and that the cut-out switch works.

Side stand

FireBlades, like most other sports bikes, have no centre stand, and a paddock stand is highly recommended for routine maintenance (and for that matter, checking over a used bike). The side stand is sturdy enough, but do check that it springs back properly (you don't want a tired spring allowing it to drop onto the road while riding), and that it's firm on its bearing, which cannot be lubed and will eventually wear out.

The stand has a cut-out to switch off the engine if it drops while the engine's running. To check this is working, sit on the bike, and with the engine running, clutch in and first gear selected, poke the stand down with your foot – if the engine stops, all is well. And there's another safety cut-out to check – you should be able to start the engine with the stand down, but clutch in and into first, and the engine should stop.

Electrics/wiring

All FireBlades have fine electrics with a good charging system, lights and accessories. But as with anything else, they are vulnerable to neglect and enthusiastic amateurs. Look out for clumsily spliced wires, flapping insulation

tape, and crimp-on (not properly soldered) connectors. An alarm is the most common accessory, so if the bike has one, ask who fitted it and check the wiring.

It sounds obvious, but do check that everything elecrical works as it should – lights, indicators, horn, warning lights, digital dash (on the later bikes), and side stand cut-outs. Many owners are wary of electrical problems, which may be as simple as a loose connector, bad earth, or blown fuse, so if you're confident of curing a fault, it's a good bargaining counter.

The voltage regulator can fail on 1998 bikes, usually resulting in overcharging of the battery, and some 2005s have suffered from generator failure. The latter can cause stray sparks to ignite petrol fumes inside the crankcase, causing the camshaft cover gaskets to blow.

FireBlade batteries are another weakness, as they're quite small to save weight, so don't really have any spare capacity for accessories. The bikes are often left in the garage for long periods, which doesn't help, and alarms will be a permanent drain on battery power – ask if the battery has been on trickle charge while the bike is unused. That's a good sign of a conscientious owner. If the battery is past its best, decent quality new ones don't cost much.

Wheels/tyres

4️⃣ 3️⃣ 2️⃣ 1️⃣

All FireBlades have cast alloy wheels and tubeless tyres. Tyre life is a big issue on a bike this powerful, and 3000 miles on a rear is a good average, with hard riders getting even less, though most can expect 6-7000 from a front.

A paddock stand makes the job easier.

Take a good look at the tyres. If they're a well known top brand – Bridgestone, Avon, Pirelli, etc – that's a good sign. If they have less than 50 per cent of their tread left, then include the replacement cost in your negotiations. Check them over for damage and sidewall cracks. And look at the wear pattern – if they are worn right up to the sidewalls, that's another sign of a hard rider (not necessarily a bad thing, as long as

Far left: Wheels must run true, and don't forget the bearings.

Worn tyres are a good bargaining chip.

they've cared for the bike). If the rear in particular is worn flat, it means the bike has done a lot of straightline motorway miles, though you are less likely to encounter this with a FireBlade.

Now for the wheels. If you've brought a paddock stand along, this will make the

job much easier. If you don't have
one, prop up the bike using a car
jack or block of wood, though
you'll need a helper to keep the
bike steady. However you do it,
prop up each end in turn and spin
the wheel – it should run true, and
there should be no dents or cracks
in the rim.

While the bike's propped up,
check the wheel bearings. These
aren't expensive, but fitting them
is a hassle, and if there's play it will
affect the handling, so it's vital that
they are in top condition. To check
the front wheel, put the steering on
full lock and try rocking the wheel
in a vertical plane, then spin the
wheel and listen for rumbles. Give
the rear wheel the same rocking
and rumbling checks.

It's not just mileage that can
kill wheel bearings – wheelies give
the fronts a hard life, and over-
zealous jet washing can force the
grease out of rears. Early bikes
are hard on rear wheel bearings in
particular.

Steering head bearings

Again, the bearings don't cost
an arm and a leg, but trouble
here can affect the handling, and
changing them is a big job. Swing
the handlebars from lock to lock.
They should move freely, with not
a hint of roughness or stiff patches
– if there is, budget for replacing
them. To check for play, put the
steering on full lock, grip the front
wheel and try rocking it back and
forth. With the front wheel on the
ground, apply the front brake

Steering head bearings live in here.

and try to push the bike forward – there should be no clonks, though this can be confused with fork wear (see below). Again, wheelies, beloved as they are by some FireBlade riders, put a lot of strain on steering head bearings.

Swing arm bearings

Another essential for good handling are the swing arm bearings. To check for wear, prop up the rear of the bike, get hold of the rear end of the arm on one side, and try rocking the complete swing arm from side to side. There should be no perceptible movement. If there's a little, or you can hear a slight click, then it may be that the locknut on the swing arm pivot shaft isn't quite tight. Otherwise, swing arm bearing replacement is a dealer job for most owners.

Checking the swing arm bearings.

Front forks

All FireBlades have fully adjustable telescopic front forks; upside

down types from 2000. The stanchions should be clean, and not pitted or rusted. Minor oil weeps aren't a problem, and major ones will be obvious – replacement is a long job, so either negotiate the price down or find another bike.

To check the forks for wear, first pump them up and down with the front brake on. They should move smoothly with no squeaks or clonks. Try pushing the bike back and forth with the front brake still on – any movement could be play in the forks or steering head bearings, and often it's difficult to tell which. Alternatively, with the front of the bike propped up, grasp the bottom of the forks and try

Visually check the forks for obvious leaks.

Adjusters may be well used!

Pump the forks up and down.

rocking them back and forth – again, it may not be obvious whether any movement is in the steering head or the forks themselves, but there shouldn't be any in either. Check that the fork preload adjusters (on top of the forks) have not been butchered by a ham-fisted owner.

Earlier bikes with upside down forks (2000-03) can suffer from cracking in the lower portion of the fork legs, caused by corrosion between outer casing and fork leg. The cure (if there is no cracking already) is simply a bead of silicone sealant around the affected joint. Bikes affected were as follows: JH2SDC44AYM000294-YM013050 (RR-Y); 1M103649-1M106961 (RR-1); 2M001433-2M009728 (RR-2); 3M100041-3M107921 (RR-3).

Rear suspension ④ ③ ② ①

To test the single rear shock, bounce up and down on the

The rear shock should be leak-free and well damped.

seat – the movement should be fairly stiff and well controlled. Out on the test ride, if the rear end feels oversoft and bouncy, then the bike probably needs a new shock, which won't be cheap.

Visually check the shock itself, the pressure cannister and its hose for leaks. Ensure the shock is firmly mounted and that the linkage moves freely. The same goes for the pre-load adjustment collar – it's surprising how many riders leave this on the same setting for years, regardless of whether they're carrying a passenger or what sort of riding they're doing.

Early instruments were analogue, with cable-driven speedo.

Instruments 4 3 2 1

Early bikes had analogue instruments, later ones a digital set, usually with a speedometer, rev counter and temp gauge. It's a case of waiting for the test ride to check that they are all working, and in nearly every case the drive is electronic. Early speedos were cable drive – if neither speedometer nor mileometer work, then the cable or drive gearbox is at fault. If it's one or the other, then the speedo itself needs work.

On bikes with a coolant temperature gauge, keep an eye on that during the test ride – it shouldn't reach more than halfway along the dial.

All-electronic instrument set on later bikes.

Engine/ 4 3 2 1 gearbox – general impression

Hondas have a good reputation for mechanical reliability, and deservedly so. The FireBlade is no exception, with a strong, robust engine/gearbox that only really give trouble if they've been abused or neglected. The 1993 bike pictured elsewhere in this book had over 60,000 miles recorded.

At first glance, both engine and gearbox appear to be completely hidden by the fairing, though you can whip off the lower panels on earlier bikes, thanks to their Dzus fasteners – it's a bit more involved on later bikes, and the allen bolts may be seized in, or the owner may not want you to start taking panels off anyway. If any fastenings (and this applies to every

Near right:
Not much of
the engine is
visible!

Far right:
Visually
check the
water pump
for leaks
– this one
has been
weeping.

component on the bike) are rounded-off or generally butchered, that's a bad sign.

But you can still ascertain quite a lot from the outside. Ideally, the bike will have a full service history (with oil/filter changes at least every 8000 miles).

A good confirmation of whether it has been cared for is the condition of the engine oil. To check it, the bike should be warm and left for a couple of minutes after switching off to allow the oil to drain back into the sump. Pre-1995 bikes have a screw-in filler cap/dipstick on the right-hand side. With the bike upright, unscrew the cap then place it back in lightly without screwing it in – the oil should be between the lower and upper marks. 1995-on bikes have a sight glass in the bottom of the clutch cover – easier to check if an assistant holds the bike vertical while you ensure that the oil level is between the two marks. In either case, the oil should be brown in colour – if it's black, or smells burned or (worse still) has visible particles floating around in it, then the engine has serious internal problems. Of course, it could be that the oil simply hasn't been changed in a very long time, but that's a bad indication in itself.

However much of the engine you can see, make a visual check for oil leaks, and of the coolant hoses and pump (the latter situated low down on the left-hand side) for coolant leaks. None are likely, but it's worth a look. Occasionally there is a leak from the gearbox sprocket (actually a recall on 1992 bikes), but this is very rare. Have a look underneath at the sump plate, which could have been damaged by a jack, or the bike hitting a kerb.

Engine – starting/idling

The engine should start promptly on the button – if the starter is sluggish, then a tired battery is the most likely cause. The starter motor itself isn't noted for problems, though if it does wear out, it'll cost more to put right than a duff battery. Remember that carburettor bikes (pre-2000) have a manual choke – the control knob is on the bars.

If the engine doesn't fire up promptly on the button, something is wrong.

Whether it's carb or fuel injection, once started the engine should settle down to a steady idle of 1100-1200rpm. If a carb bike hunts up and down at idle, the culprit could be no more than the small rubber boot fitted below the left-most carburettor. This can blow off during hard riding, causing the problem. The fuel injection set-up is extremely reliable, but if there is an idling fault with it, then it's a dealer job to put right.

With the engine idling, push the bars slowly from lock to lock. If the engine speed rises or falls then the throttle and/or choke cables are badly routed.

Engine – smoke/noise

☐4 ☐3 ☐2 ☐1

With the engine warm, blip the throttle and watch for smoke. White smoke is harmless, just water vapour escaping as the engine warms up. Black smoke is due to an over-rich mixture, the most likely cause on carburettor bikes (apart from a blocked air filter) being a wrongly jetted carb to suit an aftermarket air cleaner and/ or exhaust. Blue smoke is more serious – the engine is burning oil, which is down to

Blip the throttle and watch for blue smoke.

Not a FireBlade, but this much blue smoke indicates top-end wear.

straightforward wear at the top end. You're unlikely to come across this unless the engine has covered 50,000 miles or more.

Listen to the engine – all FireBlade power units are water-cooled, and should be relatively quiet mechanically. As with any engine with chain-driven overhead cams, the cam chain and its tensioner are vital to the engine's health. It's unusual for the tensioner to break, but it can happen, in which case the chain rattle will be obvious at idle. A knocking at half engine speed suggests worn camshaft lobes or followers, though this is something that will only come up if oil changes have been neglected. At the bottom of the engine, listen for rumblings (crankshaft main bearings) or knocks (big ends) – again, it could be tardy oil changes, but also down to the forward mounting of the oil pick-up pipe in the sump. This can be starved of lube during long wheelies or hard acceleration, and more likely to happen if the oil level is on the low side to start with.

While the engine is running, pull the clutch lever in. If it's noisy then the springs are likely to be worn out. If the engine has been tuned, then the clutch will have had a particularly hard time.

Main warning lights

Check that all the warning lights work – indicators, main beam, sidestand, oil pressure, water temp. The exact array depends on which bike you are looking at. If any don't come on with the ignition, an unscrupulous owner might have actually removed the bulb to hide a real problem.

The oil light should go out the second the engine fires up – if it doesn't, there's serious engine wear or oil/filter changes have been neglected. It may just be down to a faulty sender unit, but suspect the worst. If it comes on during hard acceleration, the oil level is probably low (not a sign of a caring owner).

Oil light should go out the second the engine fires up.

Chain/ sprockets

With the engine switched off, examine the final drive chain and rear sprocket (the front sprocket is hidden). Is the chain clean, well lubed and properly adjusted? The best way to check how worn it is is to take hold of a link and try to pull it rearwards away from the sprocket. It should reveal only a small portion of the sprocket teeth – any more, and it needs replacing.

Check the rear sprocket teeth for wear – if they have a hooked appearance, the sprocket needs replacing. Ditto if any teeth are missing or damaged. If the rear

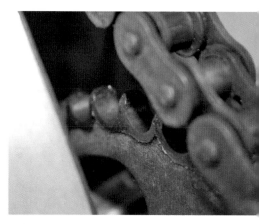

Sprocket teeth should be symmetrical, not hooked.

sprocket does need replacing, then the front (which is smaller, spins faster, so wears out more quickly) certainly will, too. The chain and sprockets aren't massively expensive, but changing the front sprocket takes some dismantling time.

A worn chain should be obvious. This one is missing its guard.

Exhaust

An aftermarket silencer is probably the most common FireBlade mod of all, especially on pre-'97 bikes, whose mild steel can lose paint, and rust from the inside. 1997-2003 models used an aluminium silencer, and from 2004 on (underseat to '08) the silencer was stainless steel, which is the most long-lasting of all. If there is a non-standard silencer, check that it's road legal (it might be stamped 'not for road use') and, on the test ride, power delivery.

The downpipes are largely hidden from inspection, unless you're able to take off the fairing lower panels. If you can see them, surface rust is no problem, but there shouldn't be any holes or leaks. The best way to check for leaks along the whole system is to hold a rag over the end of the silencer while the engine is running. If the engine falters or dies, then all is well, but if there's a chuffing sound, there's a leak somewhere in the system – it could be no more than a leaky gasket, and serious corrosion leaks will be obvious as soon as you start up.

Many bikes have aftermarket silencers like this one.

The clutch cable, where fitted, should be working smoothly and correctly.

These downpipes are in fine condition.

Cables

The control cables – clutch (pre-2004), throttle, and (on carburettor bikes) choke – should work smoothly without stiffness or jerking. Poorly lubricated, badly adjusted cables are an indication of general neglect, and the same goes for badly routed cables.

Switchgear

The switchgear is straightforward and reliable, with no particular faults. Just check that everything works. If it doesn't, the cure could be fairly simple, and as mentioned, many owners are wary of electrical faults – if you're confident of putting it right, this could be a good lever on the price.

Early switchgear includes a light on/off switch.

The early start and engine kill switches.

Brakes

FireBlades have excellent brakes as standard – twin discs at the front, with four-pot calipers, and a single disc at the rear. But they do benefit from braided hoses, which are a good sign of a caring owner. Some owners spend a lot of money on six-pot caliper conversions – again, a good sign of an owner prepared to spend money on the bike, but not really needed on the road.

Look at the discs – are they thin, or badly scored? Discs can also warp if the bike is used hard. Try pushing the bike forwards a few feet – it should run freely, but if the brakes are binding, the disc could be warped, or the calipers sticking. The latter can happen if the calipers aren't cleaned regularly, especially on bikes used all year round.

ABS was optional from 2009. It's a complex system that works very well and has no particular faults. Look out for ABS badging and the small serrated ring on the front hub. The ABS warning light should go out once the bike is past 10mph.

Calipers can stick if they're not cleaned.

Check discs for wear, warping and scoring.

Rear brakes should get all the same checks.

Recalls

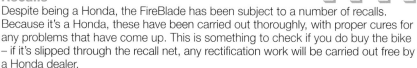

Despite being a Honda, the FireBlade has been subject to a number of recalls. Because it's a Honda, these have been carried out thoroughly, with proper cures for any problems that have come up. This is something to check if you do buy the bike – if it's slipped through the recall net, any rectification work will be carried out free by a Honda dealer.

To check whether the work has been done to this particular bike, you'll need to give the dealer or your national importer the VIN number. It won't take them long to look it up and give you a quick yes or no. Alternatively, the national transport department may keep records. US riders can go to www.nhsta.gov and click

'Recalls' to find out if the bike they're looking at was subject to any recalls (the US National Highway Traffic Safety Administration oversees recalls). UK buyers go to www.vosa.gov.uk/vosa/apps/recalls.

1992 FireBlades had a problem with the original front brake pads, whose backing plates could expand with the heat of heavy braking, causing binding. However, you're extremely unlikely to find a '92 'Blade with its original front pads in place. Just in case, the bikes affected are in the range SC28-2000001-SC-28-2003852.

2000/01 bikes had a too short fuel pipe from the tank, which could be stretched when the tank was raised. A dealer-fitted longer hose cured that, and bikes affected were SC44A3YM000001 to SC44A4YM015025. 2000/01 bikes could also be

Any Honda recalls should have been taken care of. If in doubt, check with a Honda dealer, your national importer or government transport department.

affected with clutch judder during hard-riding starts, which could actually cause the clutch outer casing to fail, allowing the drive to the rear wheel, and even the crankshaft, to lock up. Bikes affected were SC44AYM000294 to SC44A8YM015025 and SC44A1M103649 to SC44A1M105265.

2000-2003 bikes (the first with upside down forks) could conceivably suffer from cracked fork legs – see front forks section above for details.

2002 bikes had a couple of potential faults, but these weren't covered by full recalls. If an owner complained, the rectification was still made free of charge. Vibration in the steering-head bearings was cured by replacing the taper-roller bearings with later spec needle-roller bearings. Bikes affected were JH2SC50A*2M000001 to JH2SC50A*2M009833 – if the work has been done, the dealer should have made a dot-punch mark on the headstock, next to the frame number. Some '02 'Blades also had a waisted support strap for the silencer rather than the later full-width one. This could break, putting strain on the silencer, which can fracture. Bikes affected were JH2SC50A*2M000001 to JH2SC50A*2M006683.

2004 digital speedometers could under-read by 25 per cent – in other words, a legal 70mph (in the UK) on the speedo would be a true 87.5mph. To check this, ride the bike at 2000rpm in second gear – the speedo should read 18mph, but if it's less, the speedo is at fault. Bikes affected were JH2SC57A04M000001 to JH2SC57A04M009594.

Test ride

⁴ ³ ² ¹

The test ride should be no less than ten minutes, and you should be doing the riding

– not the seller riding with you on the pillion. It's understandable that some sellers are reluctant to let a complete stranger loose on their pride and joy, but it does go with the territory of selling a bike, and so long as you leave an article of faith (usually the vehicle you arrived in) then all should be happy. Take your driving licence in case the seller wants to see it.

The bike should start promptly, after which give yourself a short while to familiarise yourself with the controls and the riding position, if this is the first sports bike you've ridden. Tug the levers and blip the throttle, to get a feel for it. Check that the oil light has gone out, select first gear (which should click in easily) and set off – clutch take up should be smooth and progressive.

Compared to other big capacity bikes, the earlier FireBlades do lack low speed torque, but it's all relative. The bike should pull smoothly and reasonably strongly from low revs. If it hesitates or hiccups – and this is true right through the rev range – the bike probably hasn't been set up properly for a non-standard exhaust. If the silencer is standard, then it's likely the owner has refitted it, but not bothered to rejet the carbs. Dynojet kits (very common with non-standard cans) may make the bike run a little rich, so it'll be fine in cool weather but suffer from flatspots in hot.

Accelerate hard in second gear to check that it doesn't jump out of gear or that the clutch is slipping. The gearshift on earlier bikes is quite notchy, but it should still go into each gear at the first attempt, and hold on to it. If it does jump out of gear, an expensive stripdown is the only answer.

A test ride is crucial – keep a checklist in your mind.

The clutch should be smooth and progressive.

Don't abuse the bike, but if it's safe (and you will need a clear road) take it up to the red line once – the engine should rev freely, with vivid acceleration over 5-6000rpm, building to a crescendo over 10,000. If you've never ridden a bike of this power before, it's a good idea to bring an experienced friend along to do the test ride.

FireBlade handling, especially of the early bikes compared to heavyweight contemporaries, has become legendary. They should turn in very quickly and be stable at extreme angles of lean. The waywardness of the earliest bikes can be overstated, and you're only likely to come across this at high speeds or after hitting a mid-corner bump at speed. If the bike wallows and feels underdamped (or for that matter, too stiff), this could just be a case of suspension adjustment – both forks and rear shock are multi-adjustable, so ask the owner how they have it set up. A track day addict, for example, will have a lot more preload dialled in than is needed on the road. The brakes should pull the bike up smoothly and progressively, without pulling to one side.

Back at base, check that the engine settles back into a nice steady idle before switching off. If all is well, talk to the owner about price. If you've discovered a fault, and he/she won't make a deal, then thank them for their time and walk away.

Evaluation procedure
Add up the total points.
Score: 104 = excellent; 78 = good; 52 = average; 26 = poor.

Bikes scoring over 73 will be completely usable and will require only maintenance and care to preserve condition. Bikes scoring between 26 and 53 will require some serious work (at much the same cost regardless of score). Bikes scoring between 54 and 72 will require very careful assessment of necessary repair/restoration costs in order to arrive at a realistic value.

10 Auctions
– sold! Another way to buy your dream

Auction pros & cons

Pros: Prices will usually be lower than those of dealers or private sellers, and you might grab a real bargain on the day. Auctioneers have usually established clear title with the seller. At the venue you can usually examine documentation relating to the vehicle.

Cons: You have to rely on a sketchy catalogue description of condition and history. The opportunity to inspect is limited, and you cannot ride the bike. Auction bikes are often a little below par and may require some work. It's easy to overbid. There will usually be a buyer's premium to pay in addition to the auction hammer price.

Which auction?

Auctions by established auctioneers are advertised in bike magazines and on the auction houses' websites. A catalogue, or a simple printed list of the lots for auction, might only be available a day or two ahead, though often lots are listed and pictured on auctioneers' websites much earlier. Contact the auction company to ask if previous auction selling prices are available as this is useful information (details of past sales are often available on websites).

Catalogue, entry fee, and payment details

When you purchase the catalogue of the vehicles in the auction, it often acts as a ticket allowing two people to attend the viewing days and the auction. Catalogue details tend to be comparatively brief, but will include information such as 'one owner from new, low mileage, full service history', etc. It will also usually show a guide price to give you some idea of what to expect to pay, and will tell you what is charged as a 'Buyer's premium.' The catalogue will also contain details of acceptable forms of payment. At the fall of the hammer an immediate deposit is usually required, the balance payable within 24 hours. If you plan to pay by cash note that there may be a cash limit. Some auctions will accept payment by debit card; and sometimes credit or charge cards are acceptable, but will often incur an extra charge. A bank draft or bank transfer will have to be arranged in advance with your own bank as well as with the auction house. No bike will be released before all payments are cleared. If delays occur in payment transfers then storage costs can accrue.

Buyer's premium

A buyer's premium will often be added to the hammer price: don't forget this in your calculations. It is not usual for there to be a further state tax or local tax on the purchase price and/or on the buyer's premium.

Viewing

In some instances it's possible to view on the day, or days, before, as well as in the hours prior to the auction. Auction officials may be willing to help out by opening engine and luggage compartments and may allow you to inspect the interior. While the officials may start the engine for you, a test ride is out of the question. Crawling under and around the bike as much as you want is permitted. You can also ask to see any documentation available.

Bidding

Before you take part in the auction, decide on your maximum bid – and stick to it!

It may take a while for the auctioneer to reach the lot you're interested in, so use that time to observe how other bidders behave. When it's the turn of your bike, attract the auctioneer's attention and make an early bid. The auctioneer will then look to you for a reaction every time another bid is made; usually the bids will be in fixed increments until the bidding slows, whereupon smaller increments will often be accepted before the hammer falls. If you want to withdraw from the bidding, make sure the auctioneer understands your intentions – a vigorous shake of the head when he or she looks to you for the next bid should do the trick!

Assuming that you are the successful bidder, the auctioneer will note your card or paddle number, and from that moment on you will be responsible for the vehicle.

If the bike is unsold, either because it failed to reach the reserve or because there was little interest, it may be possible to negotiate with the owner, via the auctioneer, after the sale is over.

Successful bid

There are two more items to think about: how to get the bike home; and insurance. If you can't ride the bike, your own or a hired trailer is one way, another is to have the vehicle shipped using the facilities of a local company. The auction house will also have details of companies specialising in the transfer of bikes.

Insurance for immediate cover can usually be purchased on site, but it may be more cost-effective to make arrangements with your own insurance company in advance, and then call to confirm the full details.

eBay & other online auctions

eBay and other online auctions could land you a bike at a bargain price, though you'd be foolhardy to bid without examining the bike first, something most vendors encourage. A useful feature of eBay is that the geographical location of the bike is shown, so you can narrow your choices to those within a realistic radius of home. Be prepared to be outbid in the last few moments of the auction. Remember, your bid is binding, and it will be very, very difficult to get restitution in the case of a crooked vendor fleecing you – caveat emptor!

Be aware that some bikes offered for sale in online auctions are 'ghost' bikes. Don't part with any cash without being sure that the vehicle does actually exist and is as described (usually pre-bidding inspection is possible).

Auctioneers

Barrett-Jackson www.barrett-jackson.com
Bonhams www.bonhams.com
British Car Auctions (BCA) www.bca-europe.com or www.british-car-auctions.co.uk
Cheffins www.cheffins.co.uk
Christies www.christies.com

Coys www.coys.co.uk
Dorset Vintage and Classic Auctions www.dvca.co.uk
eBay www.ebay.com
H&H www.classic-auctions.co.uk
RM www.rmauctions.com
Shannons www.shannons.com.au
Silver www.silverauctions.com

11 Paperwork
– correct documentation is essential!

The paper trail
Pre-owned bikes come with a large portfolio of paperwork accumulated and passed on by a succession of proud owners. This documentation represents the real history of the bike, and from it can be deduced the level of care the bike has received, how much it's been used, which specialists have worked on it, and the dates of major repairs and restorations. All of this information will be priceless to you as the new owner, so be very wary of bikes with little or no paperwork to support their claimed history.

Registration documents
All countries/states have some form of registration for private vehicles, whether it's like the American 'pink slip' system or the British 'log book' systems.

It's essential to check that the registration document is genuine, that it relates to the bike in question, and that all the vehicle's details are correctly recorded, including frame and engine numbers (if these are shown). If you are buying from the previous owner, his or her name and address will be recorded in the document: this will not be the case if you're buying from a dealer.

In the UK, the current (Euro-aligned) registration document is named 'V5C,' and is printed in coloured sections of blue, green and pink. The blue section relates to the motorcycle specification, the green section has details of the new owner, and the pink section is sent to the DVLA in the UK when the bike is sold. A small section in yellow deals with selling the bike within the motor trade.

In the UK the DVLA will provide details of earlier keepers of the bike upon payment of a small fee, and much can be learned in this way.

When buying a rare bike, it's sometimes worth actually locating one overseas and importing it – not the case with FireBlades, of which thousands exist in all the major markets.

Bear in mind that the bike may be a 'grey import.' This affected some markets (especially the UK) in the 1990s, when official UK prices were higher than those in some other European countries, so some non-UK specification machines were imported unofficially. These are not inferior to an officially imported bike, but most buyers prefer a genuine UK-spec machine

Roadworthiness certificate
Most country/state administrations require that vehicles are regularly tested to prove they are safe to use on the public highway. In the UK that test (the 'MoT') is carried out at approved testing stations, for a fee. Across the USA the requirement varies, but most states insist on an emissions test every two years as a minimum, while the police are charged with pulling over unsafe-looking vehicles.

In the UK the test is required on an annual basis once a vehicle becomes three years old. Of particular relevance for older bikes is that the certificate issued includes the mileage reading recorded at the test date and, therefore, becomes an independent record of that bike's history. Ask the seller if previous certificates are available. Without an MoT the vehicle should be taken on a flat-bed to its new home, unless you insist that a valid MoT is part of the deal. (Not such a bad idea this, as at least you will know the bike was roadworthy on the day it was tested, and you don't need to wait for the old certificate to expire before having the test done.)

Road licence
The administration of every country/state charges some kind of tax for the use of its road system, the actual form of the 'road licence' and how it is displayed, varying enormously country-to-country and state-to-state.

Whatever the form of the road licence, it must relate to the vehicle carrying it, and must be present and valid if the bike is to be driven on the public highway legally. The value of the licence will depend on the length of time it will continue to be valid.

In the UK, if a bike is untaxed because it has not been used for a period of time, the owner has to inform the licensing authorities, otherwise the vehicle's date-related registration number will be lost and there will be a painful amount of paperwork to get it re-registered.

Service history
A service history is a valuable record, and the more of it there is, the better. The ultimate consists of every single routine service bill (from an official Honda dealer, or a known and respected independent), plus bills for all other repairs and accessories.

But really, anything helps in the great authenticity game – items like the original bill of sale, handbook, parts invoices and those repair bills, all add to the story and the character of the machine. Even a brochure correct to the year of the bike's manufacture is a useful document, and something that you could well have to search hard to locate in future years. If the seller claims that the bike has been restored, then expect receipts and other evidence from a specialist restorer.

If the bike has only patchy or non-existent service history, then it could still be perfectly good, but the lack of history should be reflected in the price.

Restoration photographs
If the seller tells you that the bike has been restored, then expect to be shown a series of photographs taken while the restoration was under way. Pictures taken at various stages, and from various angles, should help you gauge the thoroughness of the work. If you buy the bike, ask if you can have all the photographs, as they form an important part of its history. It's surprising how many sellers are happy to part with their bike and accept your cash, but want to hang on to their photographs! In the latter event, you may be able to persuade the vendor to get a set of copies made.

12 What's it worth?
– let your head rule your heart

Condition

If the bike you've been looking at is really ratty, then you've probably not bothered to use the marking system in chapter 9 – 30 minute evaluation. You may not have even got as far as using that chapter at all!

If you did use the marking system in chapter 9 you'll know whether the bike is in Excellent (maybe concours), Good, Average or Poor condition or, perhaps, somewhere in-between these categories.

To keep up to date with prices, buy the latest editions of the bike magazines and check the classified and dealer ads – these are particularly useful as they enable you to compare private and dealer prices. Some of the magazines run auction reports as well, which publish the actual selling prices, as do the auction house websites. Most of the dealers will have up to date websites as well.

FireBlade values in general are still falling, simply because these are relatively modern bikes that sold in big numbers. A 1992-94 bike in good original condition is unlikely to get much cheaper now, but generally, Honda's best known sports bike is depreciating in value The only version likely to appreciate significantly is the Evolution, and there aren't many of those around. But although most 'Blades have zero investment potential, the older ones do offer a huge amount of performance and excitement for relatively little money.

Assuming that the bike you have in mind is not in show/concours condition, relate the level of condition that you judge it to be in with the appropriate price in the adverts. How does the figure compare with the asking price? And don't forget that quality accessories can increase the value.

Absolute originality isn't really a big deal, and any case the most common accessories can quite easily be unbolted and replaced with standard parts. That's if you can find the standard parts at an affordable price.

If you are buying from a dealer, remember there will be a dealer's premium on the price.

Striking a deal

Negotiate on the basis of your condition assessment, mileage, and fault rectification cost. Also take into account the bike's specification. Be realistic about the value, but don't be completely intractable: a small compromise on the part of the vendor or buyer will often facilitate a deal at little real cost.

– it'll take longer and cost more than you think

There's a romance about restoration projects, about bringing a sick bike back to blooming health, and it's tempting to buy something that 'just needs a few small jobs' to bring it up to scratch. But there are two things to think about here. One, once you've got the bike home and start taking it apart, those few small jobs could turn into big ones. Two, restoration takes time, which is a precious thing in itself. Be honest with yourself – will you get as much pleasure from working on the bike as you will from riding it?

This applies to restoring any bike, but in the case of the FireBlade, you need to think harder still. The plain fact is that Honda's sports bike is too numerous and not yet old enough to be classed as an investment, with the possible exception of the 1992/93 bikes. There's no doubt that the FireBlade is a sportsbike icon, but that hasn't translated into soaring values yet. So if you do buy something tatty,

A replacement cover is the only cure for this.

Restorations are limited only by your time and budget – would you replace this spring?

and spend time and money restoring it, it's unlikely to bag you a profit.

Still, there are always exceptions, so let's assume that you have found a bike, maybe at a bargain price, that needs a great deal of work to get it back on the road. You could hand over the whole lot to a professional, and the biggest cost involved there is not the new parts, but the sheer labour involved. Such restorations don't come cheap, and if taking this route there are four other issues to bear in mind as well.

First, make it absolutely clear what you want doing. Do you want the bike to be 100% original at the end of the process, or simply useable? Do you want a concours finish, or are you prepared to put up with a few blemishes on the original parts?

Secondly, make sure that not only is a detailed estimate involved, but that it is more-or-less binding. There are too many stories of a person quoted one figure only to be presented with an invoice for a far larger one!

Third, check that the company you're dealing with has a good reputation – the owners' club, or one of the reputable parts suppliers, should be able to make a few recommendations. Finally, the restoration cost will rarely be covered by the bike's subsequent value, except maybe in the future for some rare models.

Restoring a FireBlade yourself requires a number of skills, which is fine if you already have them, but if you haven't it's good not to make your newly acquired bike part of the learning curve! Can you weld? Are you confident about building up an engine? Do you have a warm, well-lit garage with a solid workbench and a good selection of tools?

Be prepared for a top-notch professional to put you on a lengthy waiting list, or, if tackling a restoration yourself, expect things to go wrong and set aside extra time to complete the task. Restorations can stretch into years when things like life intrude, so it's good to have some sort of target date.

Could you live with this corrosion? Not pretty, but it doesn't affect how the bike runs.

A rolling restoration has much to recommend it, especially as the summers start to pass with your bike still off the road. This is not the way to achieve a concours finish, which can only really be achieved via a thorough nut-and-bolt rebuild, without the bike getting wet and dirty in the meantime. But there's a lot to be said for a rolling restoration. Riding helps keep your interest up as the bike's condition improves, and it's also more affordable than trying to do everything in one go. It will take longer, but you'll get some on-road fun out of the bike in the meantime.

14 Paint problems
– bad complexion, including dimples, pimples and bubbles

Paint faults generally occur due to lack of protection and/or maintenance, or to poor preparation prior to a repaint or touch-up. Some of the following conditions may be present in the bike you're looking at.

Orange peel

This appears as an uneven paint surface, similar to the appearance of the skin of an orange. The fault is caused by the failure of atomized paint droplets to flow into each other when they hit the surface. It's sometimes possible to rub out the effect with proprietary paint cutting/rubbing compound, or very fine grades of abrasive paper. A respray may be necessary in severe cases. Consult a bodywork repairer/paint shop for advice.

Cracking

Severe cases are likely to have been caused by too heavy an application of paint (or filler beneath the paint). Also, insufficient stirring of the paint before application can lead to the components being improperly mixed, and cracking can result. Incompatibility with the paint already on the panel can have a similar effect. To rectify it's necessary to rub down to a smooth, sound finish before respraying the problem area.

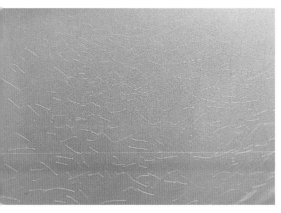

Crazing

Sometimes the paint takes on a crazed rather than a cracked appearance when the problems mentioned under 'Cracking' are present. This problem can also be caused by a reaction between the underlying surface and the paint. Paint removal and respraying the problem area is usually the only solution.

A respray is the only cure for crazing.

Blistering

Almost always caused by corrosion of the metal beneath the paint. Perforation will usually be found in the metal, and the damage will be worse than that suggested by the area of blistering. The metal will have to be repaired before repainting.

Micro blistering

Usually the result of an economy respray where inadequate heating has allowed moisture to settle on the vehicle before spraying. Consult a paint specialist, but damaged paint will have to be removed before partial or full respraying. Can also be caused by bike covers that don't 'breathe.'

Fading

Some colours, especially solid reds, are prone to fading if subject to strong sunlight for long periods without polish protection. Sometimes proprietary paint restorers and/or paint cutting/rubbing compounds will retrieve the situation. Often a respray is the only real solution.

Peeling

Often a problem with metallic paintwork starts when the sealing lacquer becomes damaged and begins to peel off. Poorly applied paint may also peel. The remedy is to strip and start again!

Dimples

Dimples in the paintwork are caused by the residue of polish (particularly silicone types) not being removed properly before respraying. Paint removal and repainting is the only solution.

A cutting compound should remove marks like these.

Carbon-fibre-look stickers are often used to protect the tank's paintwork.

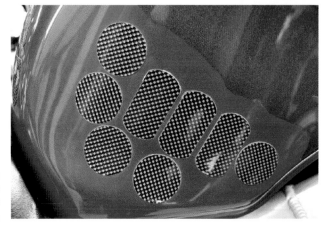

15 Lack of use problems
– just like their owners, FireBlades need exercise!

Like any piece of engineering, and indeed like human beings, FireBlades deteriorate if they sit doing nothing for long periods. This is especially relevant if the bike is laid up for six months of the year, as some of these bikes are.

Steel brackets rust.

Brake calipers will stick if left unused.

Rust
If the bike is put away wet, and/or stored in a cold, damp garage, the paint, metal and brightwork will suffer. Ensure the machine is completely dry and clean before going into storage, and if you can afford it, invest in a dehumidifier to keep the garage atmosphere dry.

Seized components
Pistons in brake calipers can seize partially or fully, giving binding or non-working brakes. Cables are vulnerable to seizure too – the answer is to thoroughly lube them beforehand, and come into the garage to give them a couple of pulls once a week or so.

Tyres
When the bike is parked, most of its weight is on the tyres, which will develop flat spots and cracks over time. The only long-term answer is to put it up on blocks, or use a paddock stand at each end

Engine
Old, acidic oil can corrode bearings. Many riders change the oil in the spring, when they're putting the bike back on the road, but really it should be changed just before the bike is laid up, so that the engine and gearbox bearings are sitting in fresh oil. Don't start the engine and run it for a short time – this simply produces condensation inside the engine that will lead to corrosion. Either give the bike a proper run of 10-20 miles, or leave it in peace.

Battery/electrics
Either remove the battery and give it a top-up charge every couple of weeks, or connect it up to a battery top-up device, such as the Optimate, which will keep it permanently fully charged. Damp conditions will allow fuses and earth connections to corrode, storing up electrical troubles for the spring. Eventually, wiring insulation will harden and fail.

Useful websites and clubs across the world

Honda official websites

www.world.honda.com/motorcycle
National sites for many countries on all continents, including the USA, France, Australia, Germany, France, Italy, Spain, UK, Sweden, Netherlands etc.

www.powersports.honda.com/motorcycles/sport
Honda sports bikes official site.

www.honda.co.uk/motorcycles
UK official site.

Clubs

Honda Owners Club – UK
www.hoc.org.uk
The original Honda club, 50 years old in 2011.

Honda Riders Club of America
www.hrca.honda.com
The official USA club.

FireBlade.It – Italy
www.fireblade.it
'Blade community in Italy.

Honda Club – Germany
www.hondaclub-germany.de
Honda club of Germany.

Honda Riders Association – Belgium/ Holland
www.hra.be
Honda club serving Holland and Belgium.

FireBlade Zone – France
www.ffirebladezone.com
French site dedicated to the FireBlade.

Enthusiast websites/forums
www.honda-fireblades.co.uk
www.cbrfirebladers.co.uk
www.redliners.co.uk
www.fireblades.org/forums/australia (for 'Blade owners in Australia)

Spares specialists
All official Honda dealers supply parts for the FireBlades. For cheaper secondhand parts, try a local bike breaker. Other than that, there are few independent shops that specialise in Honda or FireBlade parts, but here are a couple in the UK. Routine service items can also be sourced from any of the online mail order suppliers.

David Silver Spares
www.davidsilverspares.co.uk
01728 833020

The FireBlade Shop
www.bladeshop.co.uk

17 Vital statistics
– essential data at your fingertips

To list the specs of every FireBlade would take more room than we have here, so we've picked three representative models:

Max speed
1992 RR-N   158mph
1998 RR-W   166mph
2009 RR-9   179mph

Engine
1992 RR-N
Liquid-cooled DOHC in-line four, 893cc, 4 x Keihin CV carbs, bore and stroke 70 x 58mm, compression ratio 11:1, 124bhp @10,400rpm, 6-speed gearbox

1998 RR-W
Liquid-cooled DOHC in-line four, 918cc, 4x Keihin CV carbs, bore and stroke 71 x 58mm, compression ratio 11.1:1, 128bhp @ 10,500rpm, 6-speed gearbox

2009 RR-9
Liquid-cooled DOHC in-line four, 1000cc, dual sequential fuel injection, bore and stroke 76 x 55m m, compression ratio 12.3:1, 180bhp @ 12,000rpm, 6-speed gearbox

Final drive
1992 RR-N   Exposed chain
1998 RR-W   Exposed chain
2009 RR-9   Exposed chain

Suspension
1992 RR-N
Front: 45mm Showa forks, preload/rebound adjustment
Rear: Pro-Link monoshock, preload/rebound adjustment

1998 RR-W
Front: 45mm forks, preload, rebound and compression adjustment
Rear: Pro-Link monoshock, preload, compression and rebound adjustment

2009 RR-9
Front: 43mm inverted HMAS cartridge forks. Preload, rebound and compression adjustment
Rear: Unit Pro-Link HMAS monoshock. Preload, rebound and compression adjustment

Brakes
1992 RR-N
Front: 2 x 296mm discs, 4-pot calipers
Rear: 1 x 220mm disc, 2-pot caliper

1998 RR-W
Front: 2 x 310mm discs, 4-pot calipers
Rear: 1 x 220mm disc, 2-pot caliper

2009 RR-9
Front: 2 x 320mm discs, 4-pot calipers
Rear: 1 x 220mm disc, 2-pot caliper, combined ABS system optional

Tyres
1992 RR-N
Front: 130/70 ZR16
Rear: 180/55 ZR17

1998 RR-W
Front: 130/70 ZR16
Rear: 180/55 ZR17

2009 RR-9
Front: 120/17 ZR17
Rear: 190/55 ZR17

Weight (dry)
1992	**RR-N**	185kg
1998	**RR-W**	180kg
2009	**RR-9**	172kg

Model introductions by model years
1992: CBR900RR-N launched; 893cc, 124bhp, twin-spar aluminium frame, Black or Ross White with distinctive tiger stripe decals
1993: RR-P – 893cc, 124bhp, same colours, no major changes
1994: RR-R – 893cc, 124bhp, restyled with twin headlights behind one-piece flush-fitting lense, fully-adjustable front forks, aluminium finish silencer, Urban Tiger colour scheme
1995: RR-S – 893cc, 124bhp, same colours, slight change to riding position (800mm seat height, from previous 770mm)
1996: RR-T – 918cc, 128bhp, new engine with computerised ignition, new thinner-wall frame, more robust swingarm, more civilised riding position
1997: RR-V – 918cc, 128bhp, few changes, but slightly lighter thanks to aluminium silencer
1998: RR-W – 918cc, 128bhp, redesigned fairing and headlamp for lower drag, fully electronic instrument panel, HISS immobiliser, new front brake calipers with larger 310mm discs, more rigid swing arm
1999: RR-X – 918cc, 130bhp, no major changes
2000: RR-Y – 929cc, 152bhp, all-new fuel-injected engine, new exhaust with H-TEV, redesigned twin-spar frame, inverted forks, 17in front wheel, 10kg lighter than previous year
2001: RR-1 – 929cc, 152bhp, no major changes
2002: RR-2 – 954cc, 152bhp, another new engine with slightly more torque, sleeker bodywork; stronger frame, headstock and swingarm, weight cut to 168kg

2003: RR-3 – 954cc, 152bhp, no changes apart from new colours
2004: RR-4 – 998cc, 178bhp, new engine with two-stage fuel injection, die-cast aluminium frame, inverted forks, Unit Pro-Link rear suspension, radial front brake calipers, hydraulic clutch, underseat exhaust, self-adjusting electronic steering damper
2005: RR-5 – 998cc, 178bhp, no major changes, Repsol limited edition
2006: RR-6 – 998cc, 178bhp, detail engine changes, revised geometry, 320mm front discs, restyled bodywork
2007: RR-7 – 998cc, 178bhp, two injectors per cylinder, catalytic converter, lower gearing, revised geometry
2008: RR-8 – 1000cc, 180bhp, slipper clutch, all-new slimmer bodywork, 6kg lighter
2009: RR-9 – 1000cc, 180bhp, combined-ABS braking optional, oval rear indicators (clear lense), ABS model in Repsol racing colours
2010: 1000cc, 180bhp, sharper rear end styling, new colours, heavier flywheel

VIN codes (prefix only from 1998)

Model year	Frame number	Engine number
1992 RR-N	SC28-2000043 on	SC28E-2000064 on
1993 RR-P	SC28-2100006 on	SC28E-2105040 on
1994 RR-R	SC28-2250391 on	SC28E-2250388 on
1995 RR-S	SC28-2350001 on	SC28E-2350001 on
1996 RR-T	SC33A-TM000001 on	SC33E-2000001 on
1997 RR-V	SC33A-VM100001 on	SC33E-2100001 on
1998 RR-W	SC33A-WM	SC33E
1999 RR-X	SC33A-XM	SC33E
2000 RR-Y	SC44A-YM	SC44E
2001 RR-1	SC44A-1M	SC44E
2002 RR-2	SC50A-2M	SC50E
2003 RR-3	SC54A-3M	SC54E
2004 RR-4	SC57A-4M	SC57E
2005 RR-5	SC57A-5M	SC57E
2006 RR-6	SC57A-6M	SC57E
2007 RR-7	SC57A-7M	SC57E
2008 RR-8	SC57A-8M	SC57E
2009 RR-9	SC57A-9M	

The **Essential** Buyer's Guide™ series

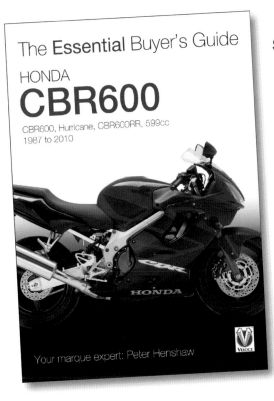

The **Essential** Buyer's Guide

HONDA

CBR600

CBR600, Hurricane, CBR600RR, 599cc
1987 to 2010

Your marque expert: Peter Henshaw

STOP!
Don't buy a Honda
CBR600/Hurricane
without first buying
this book

- Paperback
- 13.9 x 19.5cm
- £9.99*/$19.95*
- 64 pages
- 100 pictures
- ISBN: 978-1-845843-09-0

The CBR600 set the 600-class standard for many years, and was the bestseller.

Practical advice on what to look for when buying one second-hand.

Several books and many magazine articles have been written about the CBR, but very little on buying one second-hand. This book fills the gap.

Also available from Veloce –

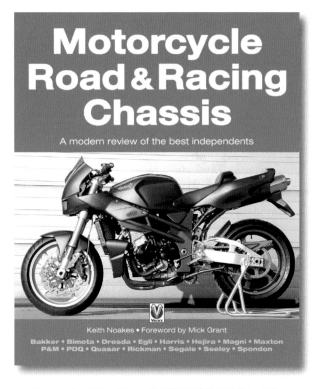

Motorcycle Road & Racing Chassis

A modern review of the best independents

Keith Noakes • Foreword by Mick Grant

Bakker • Bimota • Dresda • Egli • Harris • Hejira • Magni • Maxton
P&M • PDQ • Quasar • Rickman • Segale • Seeley • Spondon

• Paperback • 20.7 x 25cm • £19.99* UK/$39.95* USA • 176
pages • 246 colour and b&w pictures • ISBN: 978-1-845841-30-0

Cutting edge chassis design is a major factor in motorcycle performance.

This book charts the history of fifteen of the most innovative companies.

**With full specifications for many chassis and extensively illustrated
throughout, this book is a must for any motorcycle enthusiast and a
valuable reference for the trade.**

An account of the independent companies and individuals who have played a major part in the
design and advancement of motorcycle frame (chassis) performance. With full specifications
for many chassis and extensively illustrated throughout, this book is a must for any motorcycle
enthusiast, and a valuable reference for the trade.

*prices subject to change • p&p extra • for more details visit www.veloce.co.uk or email info@veloce.co.uk

Index

Alloy/chrome 24
Alternatives 7
Auctions 18, 46, 47

Badges/graphics 26, 27
Battery 30
Bodywork 25
Brakes 22, 41, 55

Cables 40
Chain/sprockets 38
Clubs/websites 56
Clutch 44
Crash damage 22, 24

Dealer or private 17
Delivery/collection 17
Documentation 20, 48, 49

Electrics/wiring 29, 30, 55
Engine
  Characteristics 45
  Gen impression 35, 36
  Performance 9, 45
  Smoke/noise 37, 38
  Starting/running 36, 37
Engine/frame numbers 20, 23
Evaluation (brief) 20, 21
Exhaust 39

FireBlade models:
  1992-95 11, 12
  1996-99 12, 13
  2000-03 13, 14
  2004-10 14-16
Foibles 7
Footpegs 27, 28
Frame 28
Front forks 33, 34

Gearbox 44
General condition 20

Inspection equipment 19

Instruments 35
Insurance 6, 18
Investment potential 6

Legal ownership 18
Living with… 9, 10
Location of bike 17

Maintenance 6
Mileage 22

Paintwork 24, 53, 54
Paying 18
Professional inspection 18

Rear suspension 34, 35
Reason for sale 17
Recalls 41, 42
Restoration 51, 52
Running costs 6, 8
Rust 55

Seat 27
Service history 49
Side stand 29
Spare parts:
  Availability 6, 56
  Cost 6, 8
Specialists 56
Specifications 17, 58
Steering head bearings 32, 33
Swingarm bearings 33
Switchgear 40

Test ride 43, 44
Tyres 8, 30, 31, 55

Usability 6

What's it worth? 50
Wheel bearings 32
Wheels 31, 32

Year-by-year changes 58, 59